How to Make Money Online

Writing & Publishing Kindle Books

Entrepreneur Series

Muhammad Naveed

Mendon Cottage Books

Mendon Cottage Books

JD-Biz Publishing

Our books are available at
1. Amazon.com
2. Barnes and Noble
3. Itunes
4. Kobo
5. Smashwords
6. Google Play Books

Table of Contents

Introduction..4
    What is a Kindle Book 4
    Where to Get a Kindle Book 4
How to Write Kindle Books...5
    a)   Conduct Research 6
    b)   Have a Sketch of Your Outline 6
    c)   Begin Writing...6
    d)   Go Back and Edit Your Words 6
    e)   Format Your Book and Publish It 7
How to Make Use of Kindle Books in Generating Passive Income 8
Factors to Put into Consideration When Writing a Kindle Book...............10
    a)   Start Small...10
    b)   Offer a Solution to a Problem 10
    c)   Tell Your Experience 10
    d)   Do Not Get Tired of Writing...10
    e)   Use Your Doubts to Catalyze Your Writing 11
    f)   Good Reviews 11
    g)   Make Writing a Process 11
How to Promote Your Kindle Book on the Kindle Platform 12
    There are other ways of promoting your e-book such as: 12
How to Sell Kindle Books on Amazon 13
How to Read Kindle Books Free of Charge...15
    a)   The following are the device options available;.....................15
Reasons for Using Kindle Books in Building Your Business...................17
    a)   Visibility..17
    b)   Passive Income...17
    c)   Insight...17
    d)   Testing..17
    e)   Feedback 18
Benefits of Kindle Books to the Reader..19
    a)   Portability...19
    b)   Affordability...19
    c)   3 G Accessibility on Kindle 19
    d)   Improved Display..19
    e)   No Computer Needed...20

Challenges of Creating a Kindle Book and Means of Overcoming Them...21

   a) The Belief That Kindle Books Are Only for Those Authors Who Are Well Established..21

   b) It is Unattainable to Get the Correct Format for the Kindle Reader 21

   c) You Do Not Have a Kindle..21

   d) You Don't Know Where to Sign Up to Create a Kindle Book........22

Conclusion 23

Introduction

What is a Kindle Book

Similar to an e-book, a Kindle book is an electronic book that has characteristics similar to an ordinary book. It is, nevertheless, a book that is user friendly and is found in digital format. It is able to meet the new demands of today's age and generation. It has a table of contents, images, and texts, and additionally, it has page numbers, a catalogue, and is usually indexed, similar to a hard copy book.

Where to Get a Kindle Book

In the present world, people look for comfort as well as devices that are computerized, which they can carry to every place they frequent in their day-to-day lives. Online websites are an appropriate place to get the most suitable Kindle book. It is very easy to find the guide details by using an e-book search online.

How to Write Kindle Books

Most pro-writers know that eBook writing is not a complex task. It is great fun and a very well-known home based business idea. There are very many easy options when it comes to writing an eBook for profit. All one requires is to do the best with extra efforts and pace.

Writing and selling Kindle books is something that many people are widely adopting. Quality is what will make the book sell to a great magnitude. Being unique with what you are writing is yet another thing that you need to keep in mind.

On a technical note, it is important to know that writing for the web is different from writing for print media. Those who have written eBooks for the media and those who write web content are aware of these differences. It is very simple to write for Amazon Kindle and once you have finished with the book you can then sell it on Amazon.

Your book needs to be written in a digital text format for it to sell to Kindle users and Amazon. The digital text format is that format which enables the reader to easily read the book on their monitor screen and the Amazon Kindle as well. Many writers out there expect to make high sales yet they do not bother with digital text formatting. It is very wrong to think that it is okay to offer bad quality and make money online. Even if you are writing an eBook, qualities, as well as, other text formats have to be highly maintained to make it easy for the reader. Once you keep these things in mind, you will have no reason to wonder where to find tips on writing Kindle books. The main concerns of writing Kindle books are high writing quality, picking a digital text editor, and also getting ready for an eBook that is easily legible for the readers.

Writing a Kindle book is more or less the same as writing an ordinary book. The only difference is the process of publishing, which is easy, even for authors that are self-published. The following tips are very useful:

a) Conduct Research

First of all, it is important to find out if people are willing to pay for the information that you have in mind, before you start writing. Take a search on Google to see if people are paying for those advertisements on the topic of your choice. If there is no one paying for the adverts, it could mean that there is full potential for you. It could also mean that your efforts in writing may go unrewarded. As such, research on a few topics on Google and then go to Amazon to see if there are such books on this subject, whether Kindle or regular books.

b) Have a Sketch of Your Outline

When you begin writing your Kindle book, it is rewarding to know in advance, what you would like to write in your book. This is because you will have an idea of what you can cover from the research that you did. Work out the headings of your chapters and those points that you need to cover in every chapter. Begin with the main chapter headings; most non-fiction books have between 10-12 chapters, thus a good aim. An introduction and conclusion are just additions to the other parts of the book. Once you get the main chapters, spend time deciding what you intend to cover on every topic.

c) Begin Writing

Once you have the above named points, you are not likely to come across any stumbling blocks. Every other day, spend some time writing. Your objective should be to write a few paragraphs on every topic, as identified in point 2 above.

d) Go Back and Edit Your Words

An analytical part of your mind is used here in editing and this explains why this is a stage of its own. In order to do a first pass, use the grammar and spell checker in your word processor. Then, proceed to read it aloud and edit as required.

e) Format Your Book and Publish It

For Kindle, formatting means ensuring that your book does not have page numbers whatsoever; no tabs, bullets, or weird characters. If it is a sizeable book, it will best work with a table of contents that is clickable. You can hire a freelancer to do it or do it yourself. After your book is formatted and proofread, you can proceed to format it.

You can then talk about it and promote it on Twitter, LinkedIn, Facebook, and in general, to get other people excited about your new Kindle book.

How to Make Use of Kindle Books in Generating Passive Income

The tablet devices and iPads are a new technology that has come to boost e-book sales in a major way. This is especially beneficial to those who use the online platform as a means of making a living, since it is becoming simpler to sell e-books through a blog or website.

Barnes & Noble Nook and Amazon Kindle are yet other markets that are lucrative for these e-books. All these are markets that can significantly leverage your income online, help you in growing your traffic, and expanding your territories, by just using a website.

On Amazon Kindle, one can write an e-book and earn real money. Kindle is the best choice if you want to sell and earn money. Having some skills in writing is the only requirement. There is no guarantee that all e-books will be sold, but what is certain is that all writers are usually paid for every book that is sold. To have your eBooks sold on Kindle, you can create a free account.

Amazon Kindle is a small device that is wireless, where many eBooks can be downloaded and its memory used as a saving device. The user can read their desired book at the time they please. On Kindle, the books available are horror stories, romantic novels, daily life guides, and memoirs.

Generally, Kindle books are priced lower compared to their hard copy versions. At the same time, they cost much lower than the ordinary eBooks, which are sold from the websites directly. The reason is that Kindle books are in a text format and therefore the experience of the use is not the same as the information books provide.

An author who has not yet established himself with his potential readers, who browse the Kindle store, may not necessarily push the price high. You will instead have to set more competitive prices than would apply in your website, which may mean a low profit margin. This is for the purposes of attracting your potential average Kindle user, who may not have heard about you. You will therefore need to be smarter with regard to the strategies that you apply in monetizing, when you are creating e-books that are income generating in the Kindle market.

A strategy, which works perfectly well in the generation of income, is the creation of informational guides that are quite particular for Kindle, and have them priced at 99 cents. This is the minimum price that one can select as a purchase price. Note that you should write information guides that offer valuable information for stimulating readers' appetites who will download and buy them. Readers are supposed to be satisfied with the informational wealth they received and you should leave them wanting to read more about the information that they acquired at 99 cents.

You can create an e-book, say about 25 pages long or so, and offer a wealth of information to people. You then need to post it on the Amazon Kindle market, where hundreds of thousands of copies will be sold every month. To begin with, you can for instance, make 35 cents per sale for each book priced at 99 cents. Even if this may not sound too exciting, the significance is that you will be able to reach out to thousands of people who may not have otherwise found your website. You may even convert some of them to your highly priced information products. Always remember to give the name of your website at the end of the e-book and point out your more expensive informational products.

Factors to Put into Consideration When Writing a Kindle Book

a) Start Small

In order to publish a Kindle book, you do not require writing a book that has 1000 pages. All you need to do is just solve a problem. Your fist Kindle book should be focused, clear, and straight to the point. Even if it may not have a price tag on it, it should be able to assist people in some way. Write because you enjoy writing and let everything else fall into place.

b) Offer a Solution to a Problem

Problems can be solved by reading nonfiction books. You should, in most cases, help people move closer to achieving their goals. Readers like listening to stories and find listening to a problem being solved through storytelling even more enjoyable. For instance, if you know how to grow passion fruits, you may write a short book on this subject. Suppose I had an interest in growing passion fruits. Why would I wade into a 1000 page book? Certainly, a book that is only a few pages would suffice in helping me grow juicy passion fruits.

c) Tell Your Experience

What makes you stand out from the rest is your story. Tell it to the world, as this is what is required. Most of us have the same desires, but we are afraid of these same things. Your story allows the right people that relate to you, to connect to you. Even though not everybody will love your story or your book, ensure that you immerse yourself in the joy of writing. What other people choose is their business. Don't doubt yourself.

d) Do Not Get Tired of Writing

The more books you write, the more they will sell. Once you have launched your book and your books relate to one another, all will get a boost. Therefore, keep writing and don't give up. In order to improve, you need to keep on writing. You will not get better at writing through excessive planning and thinking.

e) Use Your Doubts to Catalyze Your Writing

Writers doubt themselves constantly and fear that the worst may occur. This is however, something that needs to be embraced and not discarded. You may be afraid of the same things that your colleague also fears. Do not allow fear to control you, keep writing. Don't pay attention to what people will say.

f) Good Reviews

Do not be afraid of negative reviews. You will realize that after you publish a number of books, 10 to 15% of your reviews are not going to be completely positive. Such is life. Unfortunately, not everybody will like your e-book. In fact, most 1-star reviews will have nothing to do with your e-book, but everything to do with the reader. See, what we feel is what we express. Even if your book is wonderful, if you trigger fear in someone who was reading your book, that someone may leave a nasty review. It is important to realize that readers will not necessarily review books. How the book made them feel is what is reviewed. Write from your heart and forget about reviews. However, if possible, ensure you learn from the reviews, but in case somebody is overreacting, forget about him.

g) Make Writing a Process

A writing process is where one has a checklist, which assists in getting through the e-book. It will help you to focus on how to write, instead of coming up with fundamentals every time you begin writing. Moreover, it will help you in writing articles that are of high quality.

How to Promote Your Kindle Book on the Kindle Platform

Publishing an e-book on the Kindle platform is of great benefit to increasing your credibility, as well as, your visibility on the online platform. What prevents people from moving ahead is the thought of promoting their e-book. The Kindle platform builds most of the marketing side into the system for you. When something is bought from Amazon, they will send you an email asking you to write down your review. Similarly, this marketing style will also apply to all the people who will buy your Kindle book. Amazon may also recommend you to buy something else here.

There are other ways of promoting your e-book such as:

1. In your titles and descriptions, the key is to make use of relevant keywords, which will assist people in locating your book.

2. Your subscribers need to know of your new e-book. This is particularly if a free promotion is run on your book.

3. Ensure that you constantly update Twitter, Facebook and other social media platforms in which you may be active.

4. Keep updating your blog.

5. Create a video or article about your book.

6. Make use of your forum groups in your niche, by adding the book's details.

7. Allow some book sites to review your latest e-book.

8. Talk to your family and friends informing them of your new e-book.

9. Use the internet to spread the word. Concentrate on the sites that are relevant to your particular topic and niche, and also take a look at the bookworm and publishing sites.

How to Sell Kindle Books on Amazon

In case you would like to sell your books on the internet, the best place to do so is on Amazon. More than 250,000 Kindle books have already been sold. Amazon is always on the look out to gather potential materials to have them sold on Kindle, and is therefore creating a bright new future for most writers.

In order to obtain information from Kindle, most readers are constantly downloading materials of their preference. The reason behind the high sales for Kindle is due to the fact that besides being a wireless device, Kindle is light in weight, thus easy to carry, and has a low sale in the market. In order to connect to the Amazon eBook store, you are not required to connect to your mobile or computer. Your new eBooks and the old ones, which are available in print format, can be sold in Kindle of course, with the rights of the owner. Additionally, you do not require an ISBN to sell on Kindle.

By visiting Amazon's website, you can start selling Kindle books on Amazon. In case you have a sign in account with Amazon, you can log in by use of the same user name. In case you do not have an account with Amazon, you may sign in as a new user at no cost. Upload your e-book in pdf, html, or text format. Even then, HTML files are the most recommended by Amazon.

In order to have your book published in Amazon's digital platform, there are only few step-by-step transactions that one requires to follow in order to complete the task. After the publishing process is complete, you should find your book in the Kindle store after very few days. Amazon will pay you 35% in royalty on your total sales. For example, if the purchase price for the book is $9.99, Amazon will pay you $3.50 for every sold copy of the book. In case there is a discount offered to the customer on the book, they will pay it out of their share. Your price will not be affected, and your royalty will remain $3.50 for every sold copy.

A mobile broadband function is what Kindle will use that enables users to browse online, and at the same time, download e-books with no internet protocol wire. The users love carrying a book bundle, while moving from one town to another. This is why Kindle is quite popular with users.

Knowing that, you can try selling Kindle books on Amazon and obtain limitless readers in order to double your income.

How to Read Kindle Books Free of Charge

Many websites allows one to download Kindle books for free in order to obtain research data, inspiration, facts, as well as pleasure in reading. Through a database that is computerized, it is quite simple to conduct an e-book search and other publications such as blogs, magazines, and newspapers.

You may be able to read Kindle books free of charge without necessarily buying one. A free app has been released by Amazon that enables users to download Kindle books on tablets, PCs, and phones. Whispersync is a technology used by Amazon Kindle app that allows users to download any of the books right away. In fact, in only a few seconds, your book will appear. Bookmarks can also be added, as well as highlights and notes, across the devices that the app is used on and even the Kindle. This therefore means that you can conveniently read a book on your phone; you may also choose to add a bookmark and even pick up from where you left from on any of your devices.

Note, that those books which are not in their copyright agreements, are downloadable free of charge, and this therefore means that many of the classic novels can be read without having to spend any money. In case the books are still within their copyright agreement, then you indeed have to pay. Nevertheless, you will still be saving at least 50% of what you'd spend with another retailer. Additionally, you do not have to trek to town to buy it or otherwise wait for its delivery. In case you have used Amazon's free delivery service, it takes quite a long time for a book to get to its destination.

a) The following are the device options available;

    i.   The Smartphones

Smartphones include the iPhone, iPod touch, Windows Phone, Android, and BlackBerry

    ii.   The Kindle Cloud Reader

This way, one is able to read right away in their website browser

iii.   Tablets

These include the Android Tablet, iPad, and Windows 8. As such, for those who may not be able to afford the high prices or the cost of a Kindle, this is the best option.

iv.   Computers

Windows 7, Mac, Windows 8, Vista, and XP are some of the computers.

Reasons for Using Kindle Books in Building Your Business

Coming up with a Kindle book is free of charge and there are many advantages associated with it. Among them, is that your online business will be expanded a great deal. It is also very easy to have your book uploaded on the Kindle platform, and suitable prices can always be set, which you feel are appropriate for your specific niche.

The following are some of the reasons why you need to start publishing Kindle books of your own:

a) Visibility

Among the biggest retailers is Amazon. If you get an online presence in this platform, then there is no doubt that your business visibility will shine. As people are now able to read Kindle books on any device of their liking, this opportunity is amazingly great.

b) Passive Income

Kindle books are relatively low priced. Even then, having a Kindle book for sale will offer you another passive income source.

c) Insight

Upon joining the Kindle community, you are able to acquire tips and ideas through the newsletter. You may also choose to join the discussions that other like-minded people engage in. This gives you an insight to the online business world and the publishing that can be used in the niche that you desire.

d) Testing

Due to the free nature of the Kindle platform, this becomes a suitable platform for your use in testing your product ideas. In case you get a chance to join the KDP select program, and submit your book for a free promotion, this will give you an indication if your book is of interest to people or not. If you see that many people are interested, then you may use it for developing other training programs or other products on that topic of discussion.

e) Feedback

People are encouraged to leave reviews on Amazon. Many people do not do this in reality, but due to the fact that Amazon is very well known, chances are high for someone to leave a review. This therefore means that feedback relating to your books can be obtained, and you can then use it for further improvements with your future products or books.

Benefits of Kindle Books to the Reader

On its own, the Amazon Kindle is a class of book readers. Kindle got it right, where other book readers are failing miserably in the display section. In fact, Kindle displays your book just like a real page would do. Additionally, it is not more costly than a Samsung Galaxy Tablet or an iPad. The following are the benefits of a Kindle:

a) Portability

Kindle can be held by hand, as it is read. This is not the case with the iPad. Due to the weight associated with it, you will be afraid of breaking it as you can only comfortably hold it with all ten fingers. This is not the same case with Kindle book readers.

b) Affordability

Of all the options, Kindle is the most affordable. It comes with 3G access and Wi-Fi or Wi-Fi only. It all depends on the model of your choice. In fact, both do not cost more than $200, which is more affordable than other eBook readers, except the Barnes & Noble Nook.

c) 3 G Accessibility on Kindle

The additional $30 that you are required to pay in advance for a 3G enabled Kindle allows you to browse on 3G networks, absolutely free, across the globe. Amazon will only charge you if you start downloading huge files across the 3G network. Ensure that it remains free and download eBooks that are new over a Wi-Fi network.

d) Improved Display

It is difficult to read Apple iPads in direct sunlight due to complete glare; this is not the case with the Kindle devices. They do not have a backlight and as such, they can be read from anywhere, with no glare. In case you want to read them where the lighting is a bit darker, you can get a cover, that is Kindle lit, that adds a covering case and a backlight for your device in order to read late at night or when you don't want to disturb other members as they sleep.

e) No Computer Needed

Almost every eBook needs a computer connection, even if it is to be used for the first time. This is not the same with Kindle as everything can be done over a 3G network or Wi-Fi.

Challenges of Creating a Kindle Book and Means of Overcoming Them

You may have the desire to create a Kindle book, but you feel that something is stopping you from going ahead. The following are some of the possible challenges and the means of overcoming them;

a) The Belief That Kindle Books Are Only for Those Authors Who Are Well Established

You will be in for a surprise if you believe that creating a Kindle book is only for those authors who have established themselves well. Everyone can make it. You only need to have a customer account with Amazon and then you can begin publishing an eBook of your own.

b) It is Unattainable to Get the Correct Format for the Kindle Reader

For their Kindle books, Amazon uses its own format. Nevertheless, this does not mean that you will require unique software in order for this format to be created. The good news is that you can make use of a normal word processing program in order to write your book and save it as HTML when you finish. In case you are using illustrations, those pictures can be saved in a folder and have both files and folders in a file before uploading them on Amazon.

You could also be smart and create an HTML file immediately with a program, such as Kompozer, that is free to use. It is as easy as writing text directly in Kompozer, just like a word processor.

c) You Do Not Have a Kindle

You may think that not having your own Kindle is a stumbling block. To create a Kindle book, you do not require having one. Something of interest is that your readers do not require one in order to read your book. You can easily download a Kindle reader to a Mac, Windows PC, mobile phone, and even an iPad. Nevertheless, when uploading your files to Amazon, you will get a chance to watch a Kindle preview. You will then be required to check your formatting and make the required changes if necessary.

d) You Don't Know Where to Sign Up to Create a Kindle Book

Before signing up, you need to have an Amazon customer account. You will log in with it and then go to https://kdp.amazon.com/self-publishing/signin. Provide them with your name and address, and begin your first project. It is as easy as that. You only need to follow the guide for creating a Kindle book. Then upload a cover picture, together with the files, which contain your book.

Conclusion

It is just as easy to produce an eBook as it is to acquire one. There are no shipping costs involved in acquiring one. All you need is network connectivity as storage space is just minimal; the palm of your hand suffices. There are no shelves to dust, only more time needed for reading the kindle book. You can easily download a kindle book and have it printed so that you can read it just like you would an ordinary book. An eBook can be modified and converted to audiobook, which is more convenient. Especially for those people who are visually impaired, those driving to work, or even on the move. The animation and video properties on eBooks offer a good understanding of the data to be retrieved easily on a Kindle.

More than ever before, eBooks are in great demand, especially now when books are very costly. For those readers who are enthusiastic, Kindle has come up with a solution that is very rare. This device can be bought, and free books downloaded online, for a great experience in reading.

Many people are reaping the benefits of having self-published work and expanding their reading skills. Most of them self-publish, as it is much cheaper than going through the ordinary publishing venues. If you dont know, you can sell your work on Amazon and if somebody buys your book, they can also share it with other potential customers.

There is not a better time to start using the Kindle platform than now. Selling content is much simpler than it was ever before. Moreover, being able to reach many people across the globe is overwhelmingly beneficial. Note that this is a site with huge traffic and therefore not an opportunity to be missed.

Author Bio

Muhammad Naveed is currently engaged in craft consultancy, particularly, Handloom Weaving, Block Printing, and Natural Dyes. He completed his Masters in Computer Sciences and Political Science, and in addition to providing consultancy and training, he is writing books and web content on various topics. He has written numerous books, articles, case studies, reports and essays on craft, IT and academic related niches. He loves sharing his ideas and knowledge with others.

Check out some of the other JD-Biz Publishing books

Gardening Series on Amazon

Health Learning Series

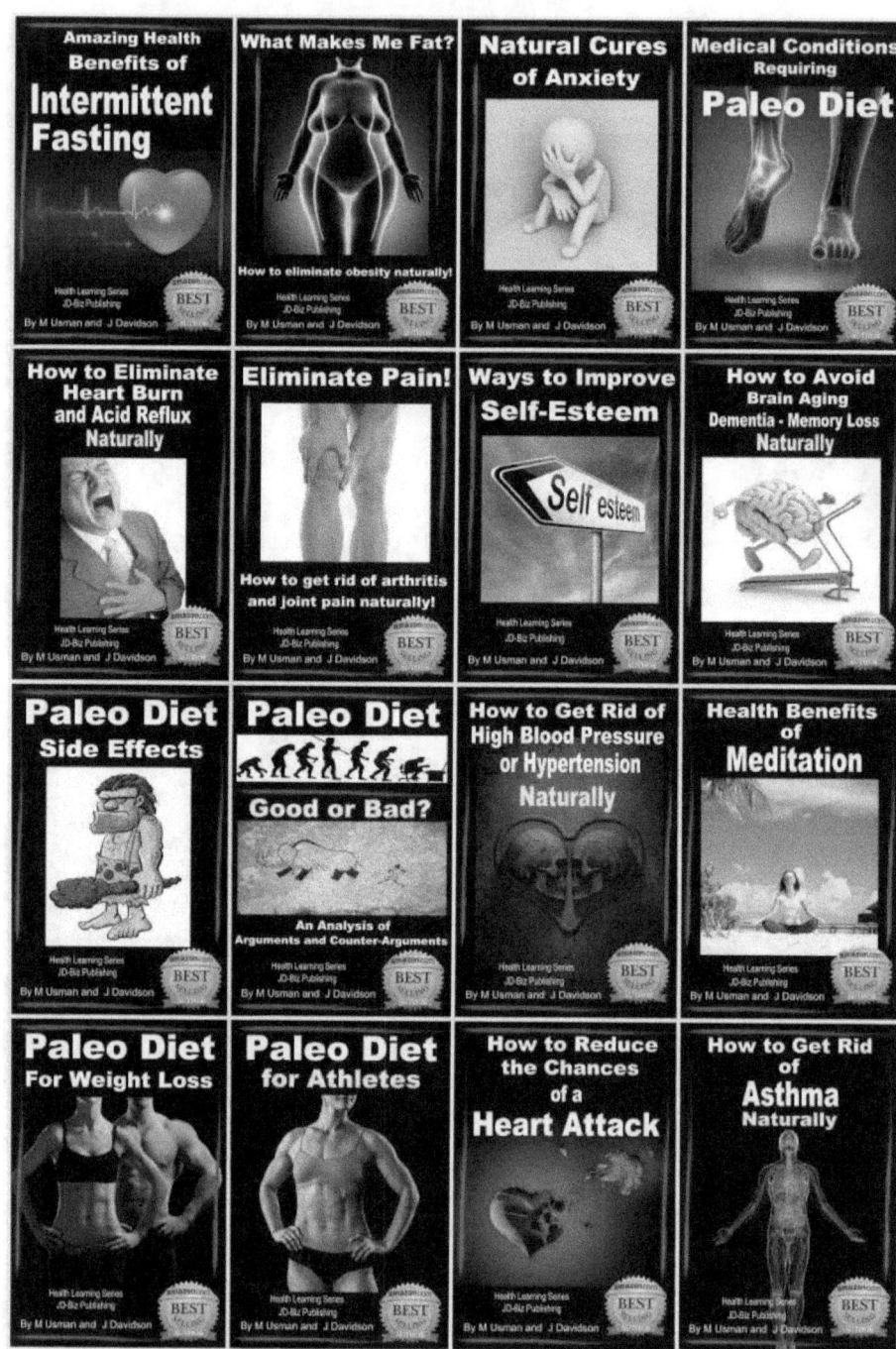

Amazing Animal Book Series

Learn To Draw Series

How to Build and Plan Books

Entrepreneur Book Series

Our books are available at

1. Amazon.com

2. Barnes and Noble

3. Itunes

4. Kobo

5. Smashwords

6. Google Play Books

Publisher

JD-Biz Corp

P O Box 374

Mendon, Utah 84325

http://www.jd-biz.com/

Mendon Cottage Books

P O Box 374, Mendon Utah 84325